FULL-LENGTH PLAYS

JACK B. LEVINE

FULL-LENGTH PLAYS

About the Author

Jack B. Levine is an author, actor, standup comedian, improv performer, and personal storyteller. He has performed on stage and online, appeared on television and radio programs, and presented at the Palace Theater's 2nd Act Series.

Also by Jack B. Levine

Laughing Out Loud: A Memoir

Primer for the Performing Arts

Tales of Mirth and Madness

Parodies and Comedy Skits

Ten-Minute One Act Plays

More Ten-Minute One Act Plays

FULL-LENGTH PLAYS

DEDICATION

This book is dedicated to **Jon L. Peacock**, director, actor, playwright, and educator, who has been my teacher, mentor, and friend. I met Jon on his popular online "Play Readings With Friends". I am in awe of his dedication to the arts, his wisdom, and his many accomplishments.

SPECIAL THANKS

I want to express a "special thanks" to **Dana Sachs**, who read every draft of every play and provided his thoughtful and helpful comments. Dana was my first director as an actor, has been my mentor, and a very close friend. **Dana Sachs** directed seven of my ten-minute plays in a Zoom performance and my first onstage play, "Skateboards and Blueberry Pancakes". He has truly been an inspiration to me.

FULL-LENGTH PLAYS

Table of Contents

INTENTIONS MATTER

Cast of Characters

SARAH WETMORE: Female, 18.

JOHN WETMORE: Male, 40.

ALICE RICE: Female, 40s, psychiatrist.

Scenes & Times

Scene 1. Psychiatrist's Office, Morning
Scene 2. Baseball Stadium, Afternoon
Scene 3 Restaurant, Evening
Scene 4. Psychiatrist's Office, Morning
Scene 5. Car, Morning
Scene 6. Hospital Room, Evening
Scene 7. Psychiatrist's Office, Morning
Scene 8. Living Room, Evening

INTENTIONS MATTER

Scene 1

SETTING: *Psychiatrist's office.*
                                              Morning.

AT RISE: *JOHN WETMORE,*
                                              wearing a suit and tie,
                                              and ALICE RICE,
                                              dressed appropriately
                                              for her profession, are
                                              seated.

JOHN
I have to be in court by ten o'clock.

ALICE
What's troubling you?

JOHN
I should've scheduled our session at another time.

ALICE
Are you still having trouble sleeping?

JOHN
Yes. I always get uptight when I'm about to start a trial.

ALICE
Is that all?

JOHN
What else would it be?

INTENTIONS MATTER

ALICE

How's Sarah?

JOHN

She has nothing to do with my lack of sleep.

ALICE

You have a lot on your plate.

JOHN

Her parents died. I'm her guardian.

ALICE

You're much more than that, John.

JOHN

I took over parenting when my brother and sister-in-law - *(Chokes up)*

ALICE

The loss was devastating to both of you. There's no shame in missing them.

JOHN

Sarah was only five years old when it happened. She's had to endure much more than I had to.

ALICE

How does Sarah deal with the loss of her parents?

JOHN

We don't talk about it.

ALICE

Why is that?

INTENTIONS MATTER

JOHN

(JOHN looks at his wristwatch) I should get going.

ALICE

Court starts at ten.

JOHN

There's always things to go over. You know, one needs to be prepared.

ALICE

You weren't prepared for Richard and Sally's deaths.

JOHN

It was a car accident.

ALICE

Where were they going.

JOHN

A private resort. It was supposed to be a second honeymoon.

ALICE

Sarah was staying with you, right?

JOHN

My brother brought her over to my house the night before.

ALICE

How did you find out?

JOHN

Two policemen came to my door.

INTENTIONS MATTER

ALICE

Where was Sarah?

JOHN

Sleeping.

ALICE

How did you tell her?

JOHN

I forget. *(Pause)* I mean, it's hard to remember back that far.

ALICE

It's the one thing you can never forget, right?

JOHN

(JOHN looks at his wristwatch and stands) You've been an immense help. I really must get to court. *(Long pause. JOHN sits)* She woke me up and wanted breakfast. I made her favorite. *(Beat)* I remember Sarah being in a high school production. She played the ninety-year-old wife. *(Chuckling)* "Skateboards and Blueberry Pancakes" – that was the name of the play. *(Beat)* Where were we --- oh, yeah, how did I tell Sarah? *(Beat)* Why should that matter now?

ALICE

You and Sarah had your lives changed forever.

JOHN

We're managing just fine.

ALICE

(Pause) You've begun to open up, John.

INTENTIONS MATTER

JOHN

(Drained) I really do need to get to work.

ALICE

Good luck with your case.

JOHN

(JOHN forces a smile) I'll need it. *(JOHN exits. ALICE writes some notes on a pad of paper)*

(BLACKOUT)

(END OF SCENE)

INTENTIONS MATTER

Scene 2

SETTING: *Baseball stadium.*

AT RISE: *JOHN, with a hot dog, and SARAH WETMORE, with French fries, are sitting. Afternoon.*

JOHN

Three more outs and we're in first place.

SARAH

You're really into this game.

JOHN

Absolutely.

SARAH

(Pause) You were really good. Why didn't you go for it?

JOHN

I hurt my knee only days before tryouts.

SARAH

Tough luck.

JOHN

Accidents happen when you least expect them. That's why /

SARAH

/ They call them accidents. I've heard you say that many times.

JOHN

It's just part of life. *(Exasperatedly)* Oh, no, man on first. Now their best hitter's coming up.

SARAH

(Pause) You surprised me.

JOHN

By coming home early, or taking you to a baseball game?

SARAH

Both actually.

JOHN

My client got sick while sitting in his cell. I have no idea if he faked it or not. But I got the call on my way over to the Court House. So, with the rest of the day free, I just thought /

SARAH

/ We would have a father-daughter type date.

JOHN

Right. *(Pause)* Is that ump blind? That was a strike!

SARAH

(Pause) What's your client accused of?

INTENTIONS MATTER

JOHN

Embezzling. *(Pause)* Retired six months ago. The guy was practically put on a pedestal. *(Pause)* You never can tell.

SARAH

Do you think he's guilty?

JOHN

He swears he's innocent. The Prosecutor says he's not.

SARAH

Would you defend a guilty man?

JOHN

Our court system is built on the premise "innocent until proven guilty".

SARAH

There're plenty of lawyers.

JOHN

What if this man was somebody you knew? Wouldn't you want him to have the best lawyer?

SARAH

I can't imagine anybody I know /

JOHN

/ Sarah, you never really can be sure of what somebody might do. Doesn't he deserve the chance to tell his story and have a jury of his peers decide?

SARAH

Are you talking about second chances?

JOHN

If he's guilty, people will decide if there will be any redemption.
(Pause. Excitedly) He struck him out! One out, two to go.

SARAH

(Pause) Forgiveness. I suppose we all need it, at some time in our lives.

JOHN

(Pause) How're those fries? *(JOHN reaches and grabs a French fry from SARAH's bag of them)*

SARAH

Hey! If you steal one more, I'm calling the cops.

JOHN

But will you defend me if I'm prosecuted?

SARAH

I'm not a lawyer.

JOHN

But you get my point.

SARAH

(SARAH takes JOHN's hotdog, takes one bite, and while chewing speaks) Oh, sorry, sir, I thought it was one of my French fries.

INTENTIONS MATTER

JOHN

Your Honor, my client has bad eye sight. She would NOT intentionally eat the man's hotdog. Oh, no, she thought it was one of HER fries.

SARAH

Point taken.

JOHN

(Pause) Hold on a second. *(Pause)* Catch it – Catch it – TWO outs, one to go. Come on, come on, guys!

SARAH

There's a lot to it, isn't there?

JOHN

What are you talking about? Baseball?

SARAH

Deciding what's right and what's wrong.

JOHN

You're wrong for eating my hotdog, despite 'bad eyesight'. On the other hand, I'm fine with eating your French fries, because I bought them.

SARAH

I'm being serious.

JOHN

I know you are.

INTENTIONS MATTER

SARAH

I think intentions matter.

JOHN

I agree.

SARAH

(Pause) It's hard to believe I leave for college tomorrow.

JOHN

I'm glad you're going to be only an hour away.

SARAH

You'll probably see me every weekend.

JOHN

Just remember, college should be more than attending classes. You'll be meeting people, participating in sports, or whatever you decide to do. I want you to enjoy the full experience. *(Pause)* Of course, you can come home anytime, but I want you to put yourself first. I'll be okay. We'll still do things together.

SARAH

Picnics and swimming at Molly's pond.

JOHN

And I'll try to remember to bring the suntan lotion.

SARAH

Mountain climbing and camping.

INTENTIONS MATTER

JOHN

With plenty of bug spray.

SARAH

You always give the best advice.

JOHN

(Smiles) I try to, honey. *(Pause)* But I can't always say and do all the right things. I mean, I'm not your mother. Mothers know how to talk to their daughters.

SARAH

(Smiling and joking) I'd say, on a scale of one to one hundred, as far as being like a mother, you come out to be – let me think – giving you the benefit of the doubt – adding TWO points for having the same blue eyes as me – subtracting TWO points for 'stealing' my French fries – let me think – I would say you're a solid ninety.

JOHN

How do I get a hundred percent approval rating?

SARAH

You can do my laundry.

JOHN

I think ninety is good enough.

(BLACKOUT)

(END OF SCENE)

INTENTIONS MATTER

<u>Scene 3</u>

SETTING: ***Restaurant.***

AT RISE: ***JOHN and SARAH are
seated and eating their
dinner.***

JOHN
Prime rib sure beats microwaved meatloaf.

SARAH
Sure does. **(Pause)** It's been a real nice day.

JOHN
Yes, it has.

SARAH
(Pause) I'm excited and nervous about starting college.

JOHN
Totally understandable.

SARAH
You know I've always wanted to be a writer.

JOHN
Do you remember writing something in the fourth or fifth grade?

SARAH
How could I forget? My teacher thought I had lost my mind. She
wasn't sure if I was trying to be funny or be a smart aleck.

INTENTIONS MATTER

JOHN

It was a play, right?

SARAH

It didn't follow proper formatting, but hey, who is going to criticize a young girl with enthusiasm?

JOHN

I forget. What was it about?

SARAH

How could you forget Gerry, the talking monkey, and his sidekick, Dusty, the talking horse?

JOHN

Where did you come up with the idea?

SARAH

You gave it to me.

JOHN

Oh, yeah, I was struggling to come up with a good summation.

SARAH

"Writer's block" – that's the phrase you used.

JOHN

Yes, it's something you'll experience.

SARAH

(Pause) I want to write meaningful plays.

JOHN

I'm sure you will.

SARAH

(Pause) You've talked about writing, yourself.

JOHN

I've been busy.

SARAH

Will you start writing when I'm away?

JOHN

Parenting never stops.

SARAH

You should write a memoir.

JOHN

I've thought about doing that.

SARAH

Why don't you?

JOHN

There are reasons.

SARAH

Like what?

JOHN

My ever-probing girl.

SARAH

Just like you, Mr. Lawyer. *(Long pause)* Was there ever a time you felt a burden with having me to take care of?

INTENTIONS MATTER

JOHN

Why would you ever think that?

SARAH

I'm not your child. You were forced into being both my parents because of what happened to them. You never got married. Your whole life might have been different.

JOHN

I've never, ever had that moment. And I'm absolutely sure, I never will. You are a blessing to me.

SARAH

You've made me a strong and independent person, most of the time. But, I guess, truth be told, I'm still insecure about some things.

JOHN

You're mature in so many ways, but you're still a teenager. College is your next step in your transition into becoming a professional author, and perhaps a wife and mother someday. *(Pause)* Tomorrow you'll be eating at the campus dining hall. I'd imagine the food might not be as good. *(Pause)* My little girl has grown up and is going to college. *(Sigh. Pause)*

SARAH

I understand. *(Pause)* I'd like to leave by eight. There's a lot to do. *(Pause)* Did you take as much stuff to college?

JOHN

(Smiling) Not as many clothes.

SARAH

(Thinking) Maybe I should take the microwave?

INTENTIONS MATTER

JOHN
Unless you want it strapped to the top of my car /

SARAH
Yeah, I guess I could do without that – for now.

JOHN
How about I cook your favorite breakfast of blueberry pancakes and then we'll takeoff at eight?

SARAH
That'll work. *(Pause)* This is yummy.

(BLACKOUT)

(END OF SCENE)

INTENTIONS MATTER

Scene 4

SETTING: *Psychiatrist's office.*
                                             Morning.

AT RISE: *JOHN and ALICE are*
                                             seated.

ALICE

In our last session, we were talking about the morning you had to tell
Sarah about her parents.

JOHN

I think we covered that.

ALICE

You made breakfast for her.

JOHN

Yes. Her favorite.

ALICE

You told her about her parents.

JOHN

What's the point of going over what happened thirteen years ago?

ALICE

Sarah was happy being with you. She woke up and had a nice
breakfast. And then you told her.

INTENTIONS MATTER

JOHN

(Thinking) Have you ever wondered what might have happened if things turned out differently? I mean, here you are, a psychiatrist, listening to me and all your other clients talk about their issues and problems. You wanted to move forward but didn't know how.

ALICE

Are you talking about your brother?

JOHN

(Long pause) Richard was two years older than me. I idolized him. He taught me how to swim, encouraged me. There were so many things he did for me.

ALICE

So, you had a good relationship with him.

JOHN

(Thinking) Richard was the one who got me interested in becoming a lawyer. Did you know that? *(ALICE shakes her head to indicate "No")* Of course, you wouldn't. I never told you. *(Long pause)* I was thinking of becoming a professional baseball player. I was surprisingly good. But, anyway, unexpected things can happen, and, well, you can get badly injured, by sheer accident, and there's no more professional sports contract to be had – so you hear your brother say, "why not become a lawyer?", maybe for the wrong reason – "you can learn how to sue the kid's parents for what he did" – or, it could be for the right reason, like protection against the injustice inflicted upon us.

ALICE

Who inflicted the injustice?

INTENTIONS MATTER

JOHN

Always probing. I guess that's your job. To get under the hood of a car. Peel the onion. Find out what's at its core.

ALICE

What did your brother do?

JOHN

Are you asking if he was a lawyer like me, or a butcher, or a baker, or a candlestick maker?

ALICE

I'm asking about actions taken.

JOHN

Yes, of course. It's what you do, or not, that makes the – what should I call it? – impact, yes, impact. Is that what you're getting at? *(Beat)* I lost my train of thought. Thinking all the time can be exhausting. I take sleeping pills.

ALICE

How often do you take them?

JOHN

Pretty much every night. *(Long pause. JOHN is racked by guilt)*

ALICE

(Pause) Are you feeling remorseful about something, John?

INTENTIONS MATTER

JOHN

Sure. I feel responsible when my client is pronounced guilty by the jury. There's no other way to be. I hold the future of my client in my hands. He or she is counting on me.

ALICE

Let's focus on you and your brother.

JOHN

Richard was the most honest man I've ever met.

ALICE

(Pause) So, he didn't lie.

JOHN

Never for anything important.

ALICE

Are you saying you lied?

JOHN

Words can sting, don't you think? A little lie here, a little lie there. One on top of the other. One by one until the whole thing comes tumbling down. At a time you didn't expect, in a way you couldn't have known. *(Long pause)* I told you that I loved my brother. It's true, you know. *(Two beats)* We were talking about me telling Sarah about her parents. She cried when I told her, "mommy and daddy went to Heaven." *(Pause)* It took time and patience and a lot of crying.

ALICE

We're out of time, John.

INTENTIONS MATTER

JOHN

Do you really think these sessions are necessary?

ALICE

Sleeping pills aren't the remedy.

JOHN

I'm not sure I'm feeling better.

ALICE

We'll talk again soon. Good luck in court.

JOHN

(JOHN stands) When will I shake how I'm feeling?

ALICE

You'll know when it happens.

JOHN

I guess I will. Bye. *(JOHN exits, as ALICE watches. ALICE then writes some notes on a pad of paper)*

(BLACKOUT)

(END OF SCENE)

INTENTIONS MATTER

Scene 5

SETTING: ***Car. Morning.***

AT RISE: ***JOHN is driving, and SARAH is in the passenger seat.***

JOHN

We should be there soon.

SARAH

I'm not sure if I'll get the chance to call.

JOHN

I understand. With orientation, buying books, and on and on, it'll be three full days.

SARAH

Don't worry, I'll let you know how it's going.

JOHN

Will you need a ride home next week?

SARAH

I think so. I'll call you and let you know.

JOHN

That works for me.

INTENTIONS MATTER

SARAH

(Pause) By the way, I met a guy at the diner where I work. It turns out he'll be at school. At least, there will one person at college that I already know.

JOHN

You'll make lots of friends.

SARAH

I hope you're ready to carry all my stuff up three flights.

JOHN

I was thinking it wouldn't be so bad with an elevator. But you're right, everybody's moving in today.

SARAH

(Pause) If I need the microwave, will you bring it?

JOHN

You're going to need room for your books and clothes.

SARAH

(Pause) That reminds me. I forgot to take my light blue dress and matching shoes. Can you /

JOHN

/ Are you really going to need a dress? *(SARAH stares at JOHN with the 'of course' look)* Right, dress and shoes. *(Pause)* Is there anything else?

INTENTIONS MATTER

SARAH

(Pause) Probably. *(Pause)* Oh, look, we're here! *(Pause)* I think you can pull into *(Points)* that parking lot. *(JOHN 'steers car' into parking space)* I didn't think we'd get this close to my dorm. *(JOHN turns off engine)* I'll run in to get my room key. *(SARAH exits 'car')*

JOHN

(JOHN watches SARAH, as she enters dorm – exiting stage. Pause) They say it never gets easier.

(BLACKOUT)

(END OF SCENE)

INTENTIONS MATTER

Scene 6

SETTING: *Hospital room.*
                                        Evening.

AT RISE: *SARAH is in hospital*
                                        bed. JOHN is sitting in
                                        a nearby chair.

JOHN

Can I get you something?

SARAH

(Weakly) No, thanks.

JOHN

I can't imagine what you're feeling right now.

SARAH

I'm a good girl. I never thought anything like this would happen to me.
People are going to blame me for what happened.

JOHN

I've known you for your whole life. There's no way you would've
done anything to make it your fault. You have the highest ethics and
morals of anybody I know.

SARAH

I just know there will be people who blame me.

INTENTIONS MATTER

JOHN

Unfortunately, some people will always believe the woman is at fault. But the law is clear. When you say, "No", it means just that. *(Pause)* I'll speak to Bill at the firm. He specializes in sexual abuse cases.

SARAH

I don't know if I can handle all of it.

JOHN

You won't be pushed into anything you don't want to do. It will be your decision. But I do think, you should hear your options. Also, you should have an Advocate, to help you. They know a lot more than I do. I think it's really important you have all the support available.

SARAH

Whatever you think is best.

JOHN

We're going to take one step at a time.

SARAH

My life will never be the same.

JOHN

You're the same good girl.

SARAH

I'm so ashamed.

JOHN

It wasn't your fault.

INTENTIONS MATTER

SARAH

How am I ever going to get over this?

JOHN

You're going to have a lot of good people helping. Bill will take care of the legal. Your Advocate will be a great resource. And I'll always be by your side.

SARAH

I want my life back.

JOHN

You will. I promise.

SARAH

(Big sigh. Weakly) I hope so.

JOHN

(JOHN moves to comfort SARAH, by holding her hand) I think you should try to get some sleep. We'll talk more in the morning. *(SARAH nods. JOHN kisses SARAH on her forehead. JOHN exits. SARAH stares in thought for five beats, then closes her eyes)*

(BLACKOUT)

(END OF SCENE)

INTENTIONS MATTER

Scene 7

SETTING: *Psychiatrist's office.*
                                                   Morning.

AT RISE: *ALICE is seated and*
                                                   writing notes on a pad
                                                   of paper, for five beats.
                                                   JOHN enters.

ALICE

Good morning, John. Please take a seat.

JOHN

(JOHN has been running to get to his therapy session) I'm sorry – I
forgot – to set my alarm – and overslept. *(JOHN sits)* I apologize – for
being late.

ALICE

You're barely five minutes past the stroke of midnight, Cinderella. I'm
sure you're not going to turn into a pumpkin. *(JOHN laughs a little
and becomes a little relaxed. Pause)* How is Sarah doing?

JOHN

She's traumatized. She has had to deal with a lot in her life. It's not
going to be easy – especially not having your mother there to talk to –
but we're trying to - *(Chokes up and covers his face, as he tries to hold
back his tears)*

ALICE

There's nothing much worse than to be sexually assaulted.

34

INTENTIONS MATTER

JOHN

I think not having your mother may be.

ALICE

Sarah has had you there to help her grow up.

JOHN

Sometimes I'm confident in what I do and say. I've taken the time and effort to prepare myself. I consider all the options, weigh the pros and cons, and make a judgment on what's best to do.

ALICE

You're describing how you function as a lawyer, a successful one at that. But John, parenting a child, now a teenager in college, is never easy – for a mother or father – or an uncle who stepped into being both.

JOHN

Obviously, I read a lot. Of course I need to read relevant case law, transcripts, depositions – you know, the whole kit and caboodle, to be prepared. *(Pause)* I've read books on parenting, teenagers – *(Sighs)* Never enough.

ALICE

(Pause) You've never been married, right?

JOHN

No, I haven't.

ALICE

Do you wish you had a girlfriend, or even better, a mother for Sarah?

INTENTIONS MATTER

JOHN

Yes. I can't always say or do the things mothers instinctively know to communicate with their daughters.

ALICE

Have you had a serious relationship with a woman?

JOHN

Yes.

ALICE

Why didn't it work out?

JOHN

I suppose you could saying timing.

ALICE

Did you know anyone who could've been a good mother to Sarah?

JOHN

Yes.

ALICE

So, what kept you from proposing?

JOHN

As I said, timing.

ALICE

Can you be more specific?

INTENTIONS MATTER

JOHN

(JOHN stands) Look, I really should be going. Busy day. You know what they're like. *(JOHN exits)*

ALICE

So much pain.

(BLACKOUT)

(END OF SCENE)

INTENTIONS MATTER

Scene 8

SETTING: *Living room. Evening.*

AT RISE: *JOHN and SARAH are sitting.*

JOHN

How are you feeling?

SARAH

I wonder if I was at least partially at fault.

JOHN

You're a trusting person.

SARAH

Naïve would be a better term.

JOHN

We all make mistakes.

SARAH

I should've known better. *(Pause)*

JOHN

People make mistakes… *(Pause)* even me.

SARAH

What are you talking about? *(Pause)* Is something else bothering you. *(Pause)* You've been like a father to me since I was left without parents. There's nothing you could've done that would ever make me think less of you.

INTENTIONS MATTER

JOHN

I'm not so sure. *(Pause)* I've tried to bring you up with good morals. You have made me proud.

SARAH

Does it concern me? *(Pause)* I really would like to know.

JOHN

I'm afraid – I'm afraid you will hate me.

SARAH

I could never hate you.

JOHN

(Long pause. JOHN pulls a wrinkled, old photograph from his wallet. JOHN looks at the photograph, and then hands the photograph to SARAH, who looks at it for several beats) I found this photograph on the kitchen table in your house the day after --- you know. I'm sure your father saw it.

SARAH

It's a photo of you and my mom… *(Pause)* I don't understand.

JOHN

You were staying with me, while your parents were going to stay at a private resort for a second honeymoon. *(Long pause)* My brother called me from his car. He was traveling with your mother. *(Pause)* He was terribly upset. I remember his words exactly. "John, you betrayed me."

SARAH

What else did he say?

JOHN

(Long pause) Nothing.

SARAH

Did you talk to him later about it?

JOHN

(Long pause) No. I heard a loud crash. The phone went dead. *(JOHN cries)* I not only betrayed my brother, but I killed your father and mother.

SARAH

How did you betray your brother? *(SARAH looks again at the photo)* Did you and my mom…

JOHN

I fell in love with your mother. She felt the same way about me. But she was married to my brother, and I had no right to betray him.

SARAH

So, my mom was sleeping with both you and my dad. How long was this going on?

JOHN

A couple of years. We both felt guilty, but not enough to stop. Then your mom got pregnant. We both realized that she needed to be a full-time wife, and mother to her child – and that left no room for me, so we ended it.

SARAH

Did she know who the father was?

INTENTIONS MATTER

JOHN

She wasn't sure. *(Pause)* I'm not either. *(Long pause)* I'll take a DNA test if you want to know.

SARAH

No, it won't change a thing. You ARE my father.

JOHN

(Long pause) You were too young and vulnerable to tell you the truth. I wanted to say something that would make sense, not just to you but to me. *(Pause)* I know what I did was wrong. I was sleeping with a married woman. I was in love with my brother's wife. *(Pause)* How could I do a thing like that? *(Pause)* I think you know I've been going to a psychiatrist. She's been trying to help me. Sleeping pills help a little. But I keep having nightmares, feelings of guilt and regret. *(Pause)* I had a client once, who was convicted of murder. *(Pause)* He was sure his wife was cheating on him. So, one night he went to the motel room, where they were, busted down the door, and shot her lover. *(Pause)* Do you know what he told me when he was sentenced to life in prison? *(SARAH slowly shakes her head)* "I should've killed my wife, too." *(Pause)* He had no remorse. *(Pause)* Imagine that. *(Pause)* You just never know what gets into a person's mind, or heart. *(Pause)* There's a powerful force within us. Is it evil? Is it love? *(Pause)* You have every right to judge me. Right or wrong. Good or bad. Innocent or guilty. *(JOHN puts his head down and is silent)*

SARAH

(Long pause) I never realized you had this pain. *(Pause)* We each have a void, a hole in our heart, a tear in our soul. We want to fill it, repair it, and make ourselves whole again. *(Pause)* I look at you and I see a loving, caring, and wonderful father. I see <u>no</u> evil. I see <u>no</u> malice. I see <u>no</u> bad intentions.

INTENTIONS MATTER

JOHN

(Big Sigh. Long pause) Your mother told me something once. *(Pause)* "We are like waves controlled by the moon and wind." *(Pause)* Your mother was very wise. She knew our choices were greatly influenced by things beyond our control. In our case, it was the power of love. It wasn't planned or intentional, but it did happen. *(Pause)* Were we wrong to have an affair? YES! But our intentions were motivated solely by our love for each other.

SARAH

(Long pause) I think I understand --- this thing that happened to me --- . I never took any actions to cause pain or suffering. I was the victim. I no longer feel guilty, in my mind or in my heart. Thank you for helping me see that. *(Long pause)* I also know that you had no intention to cause pain and suffering. You had remorse for what you did. You paid the price by serving in a self-made purgatory. Your sentence has been served. You get the rest of your life to live free of regret. You've earned it by being the best father a daughter could ever have. *(JOHN and SARAH stand and hug)*

(BLACKOUT)

(END OF PLAY)

BROKEN SPIRIT

Cast of Characters

DANIEL CARTER: Male, age 50, husband of Jessica

JESSICA CARTER: Female, age 45, wife of Daniel

JASON LEWIS: Male, age 52, best friend of Daniel

NICOLE WILSON: Female, age 55, Superintendent of Schools

LEIGH HOLT: Oncologist

CHRIS SORENSON: Bartender

Ensemble:

ACTOR 1:   EMPLOYEE #1; LOAN OFFICER

ACTOR 2:   EMPLOYEE #2; NURSE

*Note to Director: **LEIGH HOLT, CHRIS SORENSON, ACTOR 1, and ACTOR 2** may be male or female and any appropriate age.*

BROKEN SPIRIT

Scenes and Times

<u>Present:</u>
Scene 1. Bar Room

<u>One Year Earlier:</u>
Scene 2. Office of the Superintendent of Schools
Scene 3. Picnic Table Near A Lake
Scene 4. Carter's Dining Room

<u>Six Months Earlier:</u>
Scene 5. Carter's Kitchen
Scene 6. Park Bench

<u>Three Months Earlier:</u>
Scene 7. District Offices
Scene 8. Doctor's Office

<u>Two Months Earlier:</u>
Scene 9. Bank Office
Scene 10. Office of the Superintendent of Schools

<u>One Month Earlier:</u>
Scene 11. Carter's Living Room
Scene 12. Office of the Superintendent of Schools

<u>One Week Earlier:</u>
Scene 13. Carter's Backyard
Scene 14. Hospital Room

<u>Present:</u>
Scene 15. Bar Room

BROKEN SPIRIT

Scene 1

<table>
<tr><td>SETTING:</td><td>Bar room. Bar counter and two bar stools. Present.</td></tr>
<tr><td>AT RISE:</td><td>DANIEL CARTER is sitting on a bar stool. CHRIS SORENSON, bartender, is standing.</td></tr>
</table>

Note to Director: The bar counter and stools remain throughout.

DANIEL

(Gulps down drink. To CHRIS) Another one.

CHRIS

I need to see your money first.

DANIEL

I'm a little short right now. Come on Chris, I'll come through.

CHRIS

I'm sorry Mr. Carter. I can't give you any more credit.

DANIEL

You know I'm good for it.

CHRIS

Things are different now.

DANIEL

I need a drink.

BROKEN SPIRIT

CHRIS

Go home.

DANIEL

(Takes off wristwatch) This has to be worth a few drinks.

CHRIS

(Looks at watch, reads inscription) "To Daniel, Love Jessica".

DANIEL

It was a present from my wife.

CHRIS

You're going to regret giving me this.

DANIEL

I'm not sure one more regret will make any difference. *(CHRIS pours a drink for DANIEL)* Cheers. *(Pause)* One year ago, I was on top of the world.

(BLACK OUT)

(END OF SCENE)

BROKEN SPIRIT

<u>Scene 2</u>

SETTING:	*Office of the Superintendent of Schools. Painting and plaque on the wall. One year earlier.*
AT RISE:	*NICOLE WILSON, Superintendent of Schools, is sitting at her desk, and speaking on her landline phone. DANIEL is sitting by her desk.*

NICOLE

I just got off the phone with the Mayor.

DANIEL

What did he say?

NICOLE

The usual "don't overburden the taxpayers", but "give our students the best education".

DANIEL

Did you hear from the Board Chair?

NICOLE

He wants the budget to be no more than a 1.99 percent increase.

DANIEL

(Uses pocket calculator) You'll need to cut $375 thousand.

BROKEN SPIRIT

NICOLE

Let's start off with the major reasons for the budget increase.

DANIEL

Salary and benefits account for three-quarters of it.

NICOLE

Where are we with the requests for new positions?

DANIEL

You cut all of them, except one special education teacher and two paraprofessionals.

NICOLE

What's in the budget for possible new special education students?

DANIEL

The budget includes five coming into our school district at $100,000 each.

NICOLE

There are times like this when I wonder why I got into education in the first place.

DANIEL

I wish I could pull a rabbit out of a hat.

NICOLE

We've saved the district a lot of money.

DANIEL

Your suggestion to switch to self-insurance saves a boat full of money.

NICOLE

How much?

BROKEN SPIRIT

DANIEL

Just under a half a million dollars.

NICOLE

What did you include for the three upcoming staff contracts?

DANIEL

I used the state average of 3 percent.

NICOLE

That's reasonable. Is there ever going to be a time we can put together a sound budget, as we always do, and not have it cut to some arbitrary number?

DANIEL

You're the expert in dealing with the politicians. I just give you the numbers and keep my head low.

NICOLE

You do more than that. *(Points to plaque on wall)* I wouldn't have been chosen Superintendent of the Year without your help. This district has never seen so much accomplished in the past three years.

DANIEL

You deserve the accolades. I'm grateful you hired me.

NICOLE

We make a good team. But enough of the self-congratulations. We need to make some tough decisions. Let's go over your list of possible cuts.

DANIEL

As I always say, "none of these are ideal". You already eliminated two French teachers. I recommend we eliminate the purchase of the new French textbooks.

BROKEN SPIRIT

NICOLE

Did I ever tell you I started as a French teacher?

DANIEL

No.

NICOLE

My mother was born in Paris. She was an artist. My dad met her at an art gallery, ended up buying one of her paintings, and the rest is history.

DANIEL

Do they live in France?

NICOLE

New York City. My dad is now retired. He used to work in finance, like you, only he worked at a large bank. Mom still paints and sells some of her works through an art dealer. *(Points to painting on wall)* That's one of her paintings.

DANIEL

You never mentioned that.

NICOLE

We get so busy with work sometimes; our private lives can suffer. *(Pause)* Cut the French textbooks. How much does that save?

DANIEL

About $20,000.

NICOLE

We have a long way to go. What's next?

DANIEL

We budgeted the self-insurance reserve account at twenty-five percent. I'm recommending we use twenty percent.

NICOLE

What's your reasoning?

DANIEL

I spoke to our insurance agent. She said the average age of our staff is four years under the state average – younger, healthier.

NICOLE

I can remember lamenting the huge staff turnover two years ago. But now I'm happy about it.

DANIEL

If we go from 25 to 20 percent, our reserve contribution would be $155,000 less. It's not something I really want to do, but our choices are limited.

NICOLE

I agree it's not ideal. Go ahead and cut it. How much more do we need to take out of the budget?

DANIEL

$200,000, if you're sticking to the Board Chair's number.

NICOLE

I'd be foolish not to. What's next?

DANIEL

We hold off on upgrading the computer lab.

NICOLE

That is – what – $60,000?

DANIEL

$65,000, if you include the software we were going to purchase at the same time.

NICOLE

So, I've got $135,000 to-go, right?

DANIEL

Yes. I'm sure you won't like my next recommendation.

NICOLE

I can guess what it is.

DANIEL

We take out $100,000 from special education and pray.

NICOLE

I knew you were going to say that. It's the same every budget. We bring special education below where it should be. *(Pause)* I'll go along with your recommendations. You can find the remaining amount in your repairs account.

DANIEL

I'll rework the numbers and get a new budget package for you to review.

NICOLE

Can we meet again at 2:00 pm tomorrow?

DANIEL

Sure. *(Pause)* Hopefully, the Board of Education will back a 1.99 percent increase in the budget.

NICOLE

Since we have the Board Chair's approval, I'm confident we'll get the votes. I'm more worried about what will happen at the town's Board of Finance meeting.

DANIEL

The numbers tell the story. The Board of Finance has always had a bone to pick with the school system. I think they'll have a tough time finding fault with this budget.

NICOLE

I would agree MOST of them will vote for it. But, you know Frank D'Amato. He never saw a budget he liked. If we were to ask for one dollar, he'd want to know how each penny would be spent. If we bought crayons, he'd want to know what colors and why not some other colors.

DANIEL

I'm not sure you'll ever win over Frank.

NICOLE

My favorite Frank question: "Who is responsible for all those state mandates?"

DANIEL

You said, "the state". He said, "I see". *(They laugh audibly)* I don't know how you kept it together. I covered my mouth and snickered quietly.

NICOLE

We've come a long way in gaining credibility. That editorial in the newspaper was very complimentary.

DANIEL

Yes, it was. But it did get one parent upset.

NICOLE

Over the budget?

BROKEN SPIRIT

DANIEL

She wanted to know why we didn't lower the budget with all the money we saved. I told her that some costs went over budget and the savings helped offset the over expenditures.

NICOLE

Was she satisfied?

DANIEL

I hope so.

NICOLE

The biggest part of my job is communication. Board of Education, staff, public – if you can convince people they can trust you, then you usually get their support. *(Pause)* Does Jessica get upset when you work late or on weekends?

DANIEL

Sometimes. Especially if we made plans to do something.

NICOLE

My ex never liked me working late.

DANIEL

I can only imagine what you have on your plate.

NICOLE

It's funny. Most people think educators have short days and the summers off.

DANIEL

If you have the time, I'd like to talk about the upcoming audit.

NICOLE

Is there a problem?

BROKEN SPIRIT

DANIEL

No, just a heads-up. They want to be able to come to the district offices on Saturdays for the next three weeks.

NICOLE

Does that affect our staff?

DANIEL

Not at all. I'll be here anyway. I can let them into the conference room and be around to lockup after they leave.

NICOLE

I hate to see you give up your weekends.

DANIEL

It's just that time of year.

NICOLE

(Pause) Does your wife like her new assignment?

DANIEL

We don't have any children, but my wife does love to teach.

NICOLE

You don't have to have children to be a great teacher.

DANIEL

We tried. Twice. Things just didn't work out. We've moved on.

NICOLE

Jessica is a dedicated teacher. The first graders love her. I can tell you that the parents do, too.

DANIEL

Thanks.

BROKEN SPIRIT

NICOLE

I'd like to get your opinion on something confidential. Would you close the door? *(DANIEL closes the office door. NICOLE takes a file out of a desk drawer and hands it to DANIEL)* I'd like you to read the letter on the top. *(DANIEL reads the letter)*

DANIEL

I don't think we can have an administrator continuing to supervise someone they've allegedly sexually harassed.

NICOLE

The Board Attorney agrees with that assessment. I'll have my Administrative Assistant set up a call with our Board Attorney on Monday. I want to be sure we're in compliance every step of the way.

DANIEL

There's never a dull moment.

(BLACK OUT)

(END OF SCENE)

BROKEN SPIRIT

Scene 3

SETTING: *Picnic table near a lake.*

AT RISE: *JESSICA CARTER, wife of DANIEL, is setting up food and utensils on a picnic table. DANIEL is helping.*

DANIEL

We picked a perfect day. I'd like to rent one of those canoes. How about we do that after lunch?

JESSICA

Sounds like fun.

DANIEL

What did you make?

JESSICA

Ham and cheese sandwiches. I also brought a bottle of wine. I assume you want some.

DANIEL

Sounds good. I'll fire up the grill later and we'll have the hamburgers. I'm glad I bought that new cooler.

JESSICA

You seem to really love being near the water, yet you never learned to swim.

DANIEL

I told you about my cousin trying to teach me. There has got to be a loose screw up here.

57

BROKEN SPIRIT

JESSICA

Same for me.

DANIEL

You had an excuse. My parents lived near Long Island Sound. You were miles from water.

JESSICA

We'll be a good team in a canoe. Two non-swimmers, tipping over and drowning.

DANIEL

There are always porpoises to save us.

JESSICA

In a lake?

DANIEL

I've read about them. They're curious and inquisitive. We can hitch a ride back to the shore.

JESSICA

The boat rental has life preservers, right?

DANIEL

They want you to wear them even if you can swim.

JESSICA

I'm glad of that. Do you think they'll ask if one of us can swim?

DANIEL

I have no idea. *(Pause)* I read this book on people who can memorize a whole lot of information in a very short time. They use images of things. Apparently, the mind can remember a thing, like a plant or mailbox, easier than a random number like 773902.

BROKEN SPIRIT

JESSICA

You read such random things. Why don't you read a history book, or
a biography, or something of substance?

DANIEL

I suppose your romance novels fall into that category.

JESSICA

Touché.

DANIEL

I was thinking of taking a standup comedy course. What do you think?

JESSICA

I hope you're not planning on giving up your day job.

DANIEL

No, of course not. It's just to have a little diversion.

JESSICA

For a guy who is as serious as you can be at work, you love to tell jokes
and fool around 'in real life'.

DANIEL

I like 'fooling around' best.

JESSICA

Hold that thought for later. Let's eat the cake I brought for dessert.
(JESSICA gets the cake from the cooler)

DANIEL

I'm going to tell you a story about a good and honest man, who came
home to a surprise birthday party.

BROKEN SPIRIT

JESSICA

Are you going to tell me another ridiculous version of what really happened?

DANIEL

He had been sent to the grocery store, as a diversion. When he came home, he carried three bags of groceries into the kitchen and began putting things away. Our birthday boy absentmindedly put a jar of pickles in the cabinet, where his wife had hidden his birthday cake. He inadvertently put his hand, with the pickles, in the middle of the cake.

JESSICA

Did he use his other hand to put cauliflower in the cake? Or has that part of your fairytale been eliminated?

DANIEL

Please don't interrupt. Our stunned hero realized that pickles don't belong in a cake. He was put in a 'timeout' while his wife and guests enjoyed his birthday party.

JESSICA

You have a vivid imagination.

DANIEL

I aim to please.

JESSICA

You always do. *(Pause)* I forgot to tell you. I have a doctor's appointment tomorrow.

DANIEL

Anything serious?

JESSICA

No, just a routine checkup. *(Long pause)* I'll never forget our first camping trip.

DANIEL

Did you have to bring THAT up?

JESSICA

My mission in life is to remind my husband of anything he may have forgotten.

DANIEL

Don't they say it's the thought that counts?

JESSICA

Yes, that's true. But the people who say that actually THINK what they're doing.

DANIEL

It was just a little mistake.

JESSICA

You're right. The poison ivy leaf was 'little'.

DANIEL

I don't know how you put up with me.

JESSICA

I haven't figured it out.

DANIEL

You do love me, right?

JESSICA

Possibly.

DANIEL

That's it?

BROKEN SPIRIT

JESSICA

Probably.

DANIEL

Can I get back in your good graces so we could, you know, tonight?

JESSICA

Most likely.

DANIEL

It's good to know!

JESSICA

(Long pause) Do you ever wonder what it would've been like if we had children?

DANIEL

We decided not to. I'm completely at peace with our decision.

JESSICA

Children leave a legacy, don't they?

DANIEL

Why are you talking about our not having had children all of a sudden?

JESSICA

I decided to go to the park and sit awhile. I was watching a few children playing together. They were having so much fun. Giggling and laughing. It was nice. One of them had a dog. I don't think dogs are allowed in the park, but anyway, the dog and children were playing nicely together. Do you remember JoJo? He loved to run in circles.

DANIEL

Do you want to get a dog?

BROKEN SPIRIT

JESSICA

Not really. I was just thinking of him. You know, sitting down and looking around, you see things. It reminds you of this and that.

DANIEL

What's troubling you?

JESSICA

I took a few old clothes to Goodwill. I haven't worn them for years. At least now, someone will get some use from them. Or not. They're really out of style.

DANIEL

You should buy yourself some new clothes.

JESSICA

I'd never wear them.

DANIEL

We should take a nice vacation. Speaking of which, why don't we look at some brochures? You talked about doing that last year.

JESSICA

We can't afford it.

DANIEL

I can put money aside each month for a trip. I'm thinking we could go next year.

JESSICA

I can't think that far ahead.

DANIEL

I know you don't like to make quick decisions. So I'll save for it, and then we'll see.

BROKEN SPIRIT

JESSICA

I have this first grader. Her name is the same as mine. I don't think
I've mentioned this before – or if I did, I don't remember. But, anyway,
she's a sweetheart. So kind and gentle. She loves to draw. Actually,
for her age, she really does a nice job. I don't know why, but I've really
been thinking about her a lot. Maybe it was her smile – bright and
sunny. Or her art work – colorful and interesting. But I think she's in
my mind because she knows what she wants most of all. Do you know
what it is?

DANIEL

What dear?

JESSICA

She's looking forward to second grade.

DANIEL

That's heartwarming. We'll have a whole life together to share
beautiful stories.

(BLACK OUT)

(END OF SCENE)

BROKEN SPIRIT

Scene 4

SETTING: *Carter's dining room.*

AT RISE: *DANIEL, JESSICA,
                                                JASON LEWIS are
                                                seated at the dining
                                                room table. DANIEL is
                                                about to make a toast.*

DANIEL

Here, here. Lady and gent, I'd like to make a toast.

JESSICA

Is this going to be one of your marathon speeches? If it is, I'd like to
serve dinner before it gets cold.

DANIEL

Me? Talk a lot? I'm appalled. My longest speech ever may have been
a LITTLE too long, but that was then and this is now.

JESSICA

(To JASON) I hope you ate a big lunch.

DANIEL

I mean only to express my gratitude for our friendship, for the purity of
our connectiveness, and the good nature we give each other.

JESSICA

I'm getting dinner. *(JESSICA exits to the kitchen)*

DANIEL

It's been awhile. I'm glad you could make it.

JASON

Me too. I've missed home cooking.

65

BROKEN SPIRIT

DANIEL

(Pause) How did things go?

JASON

Pretty good.

DANIEL

So, you've reconciled?

JASON

Um, well, no.

DANIEL

Did you at least make any progress?

JASON

Oh, you mean with Molly.

DANIEL

What did you think we were talking about?

JASON

(Pause) She's moving on. I heard she's got a boyfriend.

DANIEL

How do you feel about it?

JASON

I have no choice.

DANIEL

(Pause) I was sorry to see you stop teaching.

JASON

My little hobby of restoring and selling antique and classic cars became an obsession.

BROKEN SPIRIT

DANIEL

You gave up so much. Benefits, pension – you know, making a real difference in people's lives.

JASON

I have to admit I've been thinking of going back.

DANIEL

Really?

JASON

I miss the students. *(JESSICA enters from the kitchen with the lasagna)* Ah, I can smell how good it's going to be.

JESSICA

(JESSICA serves the food) I hope you enjoy it.

DANIEL

Jason told me some good news. I'll let him tell you.

JESSICA

You found a nice girl, right?

JASON

Not yet. But my news is I'm seriously thinking of going back to teaching in the fall.

JESSICA

Fantastic! You're such a good math teacher. The students loved you!

DANIEL

Shall we toast to Jason's return? *(They clink glasses and drink)*

JASON

I decided to look through a photo album last night, thinking of us getting together today. Do you know what caught my eye?

BROKEN SPIRIT

DANIEL

The photo of us dressed up for Halloween.

JESSICA

(To DANIEL) You were Moses. I was the Burning Bush.

JASON

And I was the Ten Commandments.

JESSICA

As I recall, you made-up ten new ones. Can you remember them?

JASON

Let me think --- Thou shall eat pizza on Fridays; don't laugh with your mouth full; get up before they stop serving breakfast – that's all I remember.

DANIEL

We went trick or treating at Bailey Hall. Do you remember some girl saying, "holy Moses", when she opened the door?

JESSICA

And you said /

DANIEL

/ You've got that right!

JASON

That was fun. But I was thinking about another photo. I actually brought it with me. *(JASON takes out of his pants pocket a small photo and hands it to JESSICA, who giggles and hands it to DANIEL)*

DANIEL

I knew that would come back to haunt me someday.

BROKEN SPIRIT

JESSICA

You look cute.

DANIEL

I'd prefer handsome.

JESSICA

It's hard to be 'handsome' when you're dressed up as a girl.

JASON

Lovely legs, I must say.

JESSICA

Why, thank you.

JASON

I was talking about Daniel!

DANIEL

It was a lot of fun. I surprised myself when I agreed to do it.

JESSICA

You were a sweetheart. When I told you it was a charity event, you agreed.

DANIEL

To be honest, it was a chance to get to know you better.

JASON

I thought my fixup sealed the deal.

DANIEL

There had to be some courting.

JESSICA

What was that "you had me at hello" movie?

BROKEN SPIRIT

JASON

'Jerry McGuire'.

JESSICA

I loved that movie.

DANIEL

You had a big crush on Tom Cruise.

JESSICA

What girl wouldn't?

DANIEL

Don't you think I look as good as him?

JESSICA

You'll always be my favorite. Does anybody want some more lasagna?

DANIEL

I want to save room for dessert.

JESSICA

(To JASON) He always wants his dessert.

DANIEL

Don't let me rush you. We can wait a bit. ONE --- TWO --- THREE --- FOUR --- FIVE. Okay, we waited.

JESSICA

I'll get the dessert. *(JESSICA exits to kitchen)*

JASON

Great meal. She's amazing. You've got a keeper.

DANIEL

Oh, I know. I know.

BROKEN SPIRIT

JASON

Haven't you guys been out to the lake?

DANIEL

Yeah, of course. Why do you ask?

JASON

She doesn't have any tan.

DANIEL

It's my workload. We've only gone a couple of times.

JASON

We should all go together. We could rent a pontoon and spend the afternoon on the lake.

DANIEL

I'd like that.

JESSICA

(JESSICA enters with coffee and two strawberry shortcakes on a tray) That might be nice. *(JESSICA hands one to DANIEL and one to JASON)* You fellows go ahead and eat. *(DANIEL and JASON start eating)*

DANIEL

(Pause) Do you remember picking apples at that farm – what was the name of it? Oh yes, Miller's Farm. You ended up making an apple pie and a few jars of apple jelly.

JASON

That jar of apple jelly you gave me was the best I've ever eaten.

JESSICA

(Long pause) It's nice to have memories.

BROKEN SPIRIT

DANIEL

(To JASON) We went on this wagon ride. Out to a big field of sunflowers. *(To JESSICA)* I love the photo of us in front of them. *(To JASON)* Without even asking, this elderly guy offered to take our photo. He said, "life with your sweetheart is better than the sunshine you see in sunflowers". I just had to ask him how long he was married to the lady next to him. He said, "two weeks". It's funny. I thought he'd say forty or fifty years. But both of them had lost their spouses and found each other in their 'second life'.

JASON

Miller's Farm makes the most delicious ice cream. We had to stay in line for almost an hour, but it was worth it.

DANIEL

(To JESSICA, laughing) It's a lucky thing you had those wipes in your purse. We should've gotten the ice cream in cups, not cones.

JESSICA

I always aim to support whatever you do.

JASON

(Pause) Both of you gave me the support I needed when things fell apart with Molly.

DANIEL

Now, don't you go sentimental on us.

JASON

I'm just saying.

JESSICA

It's true. We've always been there for each other.

DANIEL
And nothing's going to ever change that.

(BLACK OUT)

(END OF SCENE)

BROKEN SPIRIT

Scene 5

SETTING: *The bar.*

AT RISE: *DANIEL is seated at the bar looking at the audience.*

DANIEL

Then it all started to fall apart when Jess said to me, "I have cancer". The next six months were tough on Jess. She had significant weight loss and began to lose her hair from chemotherapy. She had to take a sabbatical from work. *(Lights out on the bar and up on the Carter's kitchen. Six months earlier. JESSICA is seated at the kitchen table. She's wearing a kerchief. DANIEL moves to the stove)*

DANIEL

You know, I might get to go on one of those TV shows.

JESSICA

Which one?

DANIEL

A cooking show, of course. You're going to be impressed. I've made scrambled eggs, microwaved bacon, put on a pot of coffee.

JESSICA

I appreciate you making breakfast. I really do. But you didn't have to do it. I'm still capable.

DANIEL

Of course, you are. The question is: Am I? *(DANIEL brings over a plate of food for JESSICA and stands over her in anticipation of her reaction)*

BROKEN SPIRIT

JESSICA

Are you going to stand there while I eat?

DANIEL

I just want to make sure.

JESSICA

Let me see: The eggs look like eggs. The coffee seems to be hot. The bacon is burnt to a crisp.

DANIEL

Is it too much? I can make some new bacon.

JESSICA

I'm pulling your leg. Get yourself a plate of food and stop hovering.

DANIEL

Would you like some orange juice?

JESSICA

I appreciate all you're doing, but I'm really not very hungry.

DANIEL

I can make pancakes. Well, not as good as you.

JESSICA

Here, take my plate.

DANIEL

(DANIEL gets his own plate of food and sits) I made plenty. Just leave your plate where it is. Maybe you'll get a little hungry watching me eat.

JESSICA

I don't think so. But you go ahead and eat.

DANIEL

You know what? I think I'll stay home today. We can go to the park and enjoy the beautiful weather.

JESSICA

I know you're busy at work this time of year. And I'm really a little tired and would like to rest. We can do it some other time. Okay?

DANIEL

What about a canoe ride? I can do all the work. You can sit and look at the scenery.

JESSICA

Sounds like a good plan – just not today.

DANIEL

Whatever you want. I'm not trying to push you /

JESSICA

/ I know. We just have to face reality. My energy is not what it used to be. The chemo takes a lot out of me.

DANIEL

How about some water?

JESSICA

Yes, please. *(DANIEL gets a bottle of water)* I have a favor to ask.

DANIEL

Anything.

JESSICA

I have three prescriptions at the pharmacy. Could you get them on your way home?

BROKEN SPIRIT

DANIEL

I'll pick them up as soon as the pharmacy opens and bring them to you.

JESSICA

No need to do that. I have enough for today. Just need them for tomorrow.

DANIEL

Are you sure?

JESSICA

Yes. *(Pause)* Do you have enough money?

DANIEL

I can use my credit card.

JESSICA

How much do we owe now?

DANIEL

You needn't worried about money. That's my job.

JESSICA

You're carrying a lot on your shoulders.

DANIEL

(Pause) If you need to go someplace, don't hesitate to call me.

JESSICA

Where would I go?

DANIEL

I feel badly that I've got to take your car.

JESSICA

The accident wasn't your fault. *(Pause)* How's the knee?

BROKEN SPIRIT

DANIEL

I can't run the four-minute mile. *(Pause)* Look, what you have is serious. I've got a few bruises.

JESSICA

You don't have to be brave with me.

DANIEL

I'm not brave.

JESSICA

Are you taking the pills the doctor prescribed?

DANIEL

I picked up some Tylenol.

JESSICA

You're doing that because we went over the prescription drug limit, right?

DANIEL

You don't need to spend one second worrying.

JESSICA

(Pause) Aren't you going to be late for work?

DANIEL

I'm okay. Just want to spend time with you.

JESSICA

I'm not going anywhere.

DANIEL

I want you to get the best medical care possible. We're not going to worry about costs.

BROKEN SPIRIT

JESSICA

I know that's how you feel. But if things continue to get worse, there's no sense in spending all that money.

DANIEL

I won't do a cost-benefit analysis on your life.

JESSICA

Don't forget my medicine.

DANIEL

You didn't eat anything.

JESSICA

Maybe later. I need to lie down, and you need to go to work.

(BLACK OUT)

(END OF SCENE)

BROKEN SPIRIT

<u>Scene 6</u>

SETTING: *Park bench.*

AT RISE: *DANIEL and JASON
                                             are sitting on a park
                                             bench.*

DANIEL

I guess this might be a strange place for two guys to meet.

JASON

How so?

DANIEL

I'm just used to being on this bench with Jess.

JASON

I don't see anything on this bench that limits it to only a guy and gal.

DANIEL

We could be here to exchange drugs for money.

JASON

You always break me up.

DANIEL

Don't you think I'd take drugs?

JASON

Prescription, yes. Marijuana, cocaine – that sort of thing, absolutely
not.

DANIEL

You don't think 'bean-counters' take drugs?

80

BROKEN SPIRIT

JASON

You're the world's straightest straight shooter.

DANIEL

I may have been.

JASON

Are you telling me there's a change in your personality?

DANIEL

I'm not sure.

JASON

Jessica's cancer is being taken care of by the doctors, people who know how to handle these things. I know you're concerned about the finances, but you've got a good job. In time, all the bills will be paid off.

DANIEL

(Pause) You started drinking when your wife walked away, right?

JASON

I drank to ease my pain.

DANIEL

Did it help?

JASON

I was not eating healthy; my sleeping pattern was erratic; and I was making a fool of myself.

DANIEL

You were drinking a lot.

JASON

I don't remember much. It's a blur in my memory.

BROKEN SPIRIT

DANIEL

You were doing drugs.

JASON

I finally went to rehab.

DANIEL

Really? When?

JASON

I told you that I was going out to Phoenix to try to reconnect with Molly. I lied. I went there to dry out. Nicole was very supportive. But I knew I had to leave my teaching job, so I used my love of antique and classic cars as an excuse. Nicole told me that I could come back to the school district when I was fully recovered.

DANIEL

We've always shared everything. Why not this?

JASON

I was afraid of what you would think.

DANIEL

Why are you telling me now?

JASON

We were all devastated when we found out about Jessica. *(Long pause)*

DANIEL

Go on.

JASON

I'm seeing my best friend start to go down a rabbit hole.

BROKEN SPIRIT

DANIEL

How did you come to that conclusion?

JASON

It's little things – at least at this point.

DANIEL

You're talking in riddles.

JASON

Take last Saturday. We were on the sixth hole. You hit your ball in the sand trap. You took the club and pounded on a tree in frustration. It was a way-over-top reaction. Don't you think?

DANIEL

One time, in all the years I've been playing, and you have to bring it up as some type of psychotic behavior on my part.

JASON

You know what I'm trying to tell you.

DANIEL

(Long pause) You're right. Yesterday, I yelled at Jess for putting her glass in the sink and not in the dishwasher. Can you imagine?

JASON

(Pause) I can smell liquor on your breath. It's seven thirty in the morning. Are you drinking your breakfast?

DANIEL

I took a little 'booster shot' to help me have this conversation.

BROKEN SPIRIT

JASON

You have to drink to talk to me? *(Pause)* I started drinking back in college. It got worse as I lived through an unhappy marriage. But you know it's all excuses. Drinking can be addictive. I can see you beginning to take 'just one more'. I'm worried about you.

DANIEL

Worry about Jess. I'm fine.

(BLACK OUT)

(END OF SCENE)

BROKEN SPIRIT

Scene 7

SETTING: *The Bar.*

AT RISE: *DANIEL is on a bar stool looking at the audience.*

DANIEL

Over the next three months, there were so many problems going through my mind. I started to lose focus. *(Lights out on bar and lights up on district offices' conference room. Three months earlier. DANIEL, EMPLOYEES #1 and #2 are seated at the conference table)*

EMPLOYEE #1

I have good news. The budget spreadsheet is all set.

DANIEL

Did you include the three new positions?

EMPLOYEE #1

Didn't you say to cut all the new staff requests?

DANIEL

There should be one special education teacher and two paraprofessionals.

EMPLOYEE #1

I'll make the change.

DANIEL

(Pause) How many of our staff are close to, or at, retirement?

EMPLOYEE #2

There's six.

BROKEN SPIRIT

DANIEL

Did you put $100,000 of savings in the budget from replacing them at a lower salary?

EMPLOYEE #2

I used $75,000.

DANIEL

Where did you get that figure?

EMPLOYEE #2

You gave it to me.

DANIEL

(Pause) -

EMPLOYEE #1

(Long pause) We heard about Jessica. The whole staff is so sorry.

DANIEL

(Pause) Do you remember the first year I was here. We had everything all set to be presented to the Board of Education. Two hours before the meeting, we had to re-do portions of the budget packages. I can remember literally running from the copier room with a box of ten new sets of materials, up three flights of stairs to the Board Room. I made it just as the Board Chair asked everybody to stand for the Pledge of Allegiance. There wasn't even one mistake in that budget.

EMPLOYEE #2

You have to deal with --- I mean, there are other things to think about.

EMPLOYEE #1

Maybe, when the budget is finished, you and your wife can go spend some time at your condo. I remember you showing us those beautiful photos of the sunsets.

BROKEN SPIRIT

DANIEL

There's no way we can get away to our condo now.

EMPLOYEE #1

What can we do to help?

DANIEL

(Long pause) That's what the guy who plowed into my car said. I wanted to say, "maybe you should've stayed home instead of driving your car without a license, intoxicated" --- but I just said nothing. *(Pause)* Do either of you play golf?

EMPLOYEE #1

I like playing tennis. Golf is definitely something that I would find frustrating.

DANIEL

Why is that?

EMPLOYEE #1

I have no patience waiting for other players to take their shots.

DANIEL

Golf is a game of precision. You're hitting a little ball, so it goes into a little hole. It's like the budget. The numbers have to be right, like your golf shot has to be on-target. *(Long pause)* My first job out of college was working as a Budget Analyst. The department head's office was directly across from my desk. I always wondered what happened behind closed doors when he met with various people. One day I got called into his office, with my supervisor. We were there to discuss a report I had put together. Anyway, when we were finishing up, I told him that he seemed so calm all the time. I'll never forgot what he told me: "I had a boss once who yelled at me for something I did wrong. I promised myself, no matter what happened, I would never, ever do that to someone else". Both of you have had to put up with some unfair outbursts from me.

EMPLOYEE #2

There's no need to apologize.

EMPLOYEE #1

Do you get a chance to relax when you go home?

DANIEL

(Long pause) Relax? I saw this commercial last night. The announcer talked about the benefits of purchasing this aerobics exercise video. Supposedly, you'll get peace, tranquility, and good health, for only $79.99. What a racket.

EMPLOYEE #1

Did you buy it?

DANIEL

No. *(Pause)* Would you make those corrections? We can reconvene after lunch to take another look at the budget. *(EMPLOYEE #1 and EMPLOYEE #2 exit. DANIEL reaches into his jacket pocket and pulls out a small bottle of liquor and drinks it)*

(BLACK OUT)

(END OF SCENE)

BROKEN SPIRIT

Scene 8

SETTING: *Doctor's office.*

AT RISE: *LEIGH HOLT, an oncologist, is sitting behind a desk. DANIEL and JESSICA are seated in front of the desk.*

LEIGH

(To JESSICA) How are you doing today?

JESSICA

I guess we're both nervous.

LEIGH

I don't like to prolong telling my patient the results. I know you're on edge. It's to be expected. Unfortunately, the news is not as good as I had hoped. The PET exam shows the cancer has spread. We're going to need to be more aggressive with your chemo.

JESSICA

Oh.

DANIEL

(To LEIGH) I thought you said the chemo was pretty strong. Is there something stronger?

LEIGH

All patients are different. There are many forms of cancer. What we do and when we do it depends upon many factors.

JESSICA

I trust you, Dr. Holt. Whatever you say I should do, I'll do it.

BROKEN SPIRIT

LEIGH

We need to do some blood tests to check your kidney and liver functions to be sure your body is ready to continue chemotherapy.

DANIEL

Isn't there some other treatment available? I was reading an article just a few days ago. A doctor in South America says his medical treatment has a ninety-seven percent recovery rate for stage 4 cancer patients.

LEIGH

Where did you see this article?

DANIEL

I read it on the internet. I looked up 'new cancer treatments'. There was a website for this doctor – I think his name is Benson. It's experimental at this point.

LEIGH

I'm not sure whether or not this particular person has a license to practice. These 'doctors' – or whatever they are – prey on the vulnerability of desperate people who will try anything. And frankly, there's no indication it works, or it would be approved by the F.D.A.

JESSICA

(To DANIEL) I trust I'm getting the best medical care possible.

DANIEL

(To LEIGH) I'm only looking for what might be available if the stronger drugs don't work.

LEIGH

(To JESSICA) The ultimate decision is yours. I won't endorse any procedure not backed by the FDA. It would be illegal in the United States. I'm afraid there are different standards in other countries. *(Continued)*

BROKEN SPIRIT

LEIGH (Continued)

And, I must say, it would be highly unlikely any treatment would be 97 percent effective. This person is talking about patients who have stage 4 cancer. So the cancer has spread from its origin to other parts of the body.

DANIEL

Wasn't it Einstein who had his relativity theory initially rejected by other physicists?   Maybe this doctor is unknown to you and your colleagues but has found the answer to curing cancer.

JESSICA

(To LEIGH) I'm scared.

LEIGH

You're going through a lot. We need to stay positive.

JESSICA

When will I get the blood tests?

LEIGH

I'd like to bring you into the hospital for a few days. May I schedule you to go to Howard's Medical Center next Tuesday?

JESSICA

(To DANIEL) Can you drive me?

DANIEL

(To LEIGH) What time?

LEIGH

I only schedule the date. The hospital will contact Jessica the day before with the time to come in.

DANIEL

(To JESSICA) I'll make whatever arrangements are necessary.

BROKEN SPIRIT

LEIGH

(To JESSICA) I know your energy level is down and your appetite is not there. But I'd like you to do your best to eat. Before you leave, the nutritionist will give you a list of foods that should be easier for you to digest.

JESSICA

I appreciate it, Doctor.

LEIGH

(To DANIEL)   The experimental therapies you're finding on the internet may seem promising, but they're not. I'm concerned that Jessica could be subjected to something that could potentially harm her. At best, it's very unlikely it will help.

JESSICA

We're going to do what you say is best.

DANIEL

(To LEIGH)   There's no harm in me researching stuff. I feel we're counting on something that hasn't beaten the cancer. It doesn't seem wise to hold off on at least taking a look at options.

LEIGH

(To JESSICA) Would you promise that before you decide to change what we're doing here, you'll speak to me first?

JESSICA

I'm not planning to make any changes.

DANIEL

I'm just doing research. There's no harm in that.

LEIGH

(To JESSICA) Don't forget to ask the nutritionist for that food list. And I'll see you at the hospital on Tuesday.

JESSICA
Thank you, Dr. Holt.

DANIEL
(To LEIGH) When I get more information, I'll share it with you, Doctor. I'm sure we can all learn more.

(BLACK OUT)

(END OF SCENE)

BROKEN SPIRIT

Scene 9

SETTING: *The Bar.*

AT RISE: *DANIEL looks at the*
                                             audience.

DANIEL

A month later, I was desperate to borrow money. *(Lights out on the bar and lights up on the bank office. Two months earlier. LOAN OFFICER is working at his computer. DANIEL moves into the scene)*

DANIEL

Good morning. I'm a little early. Can you see me now?

LOAN OFFICER

Oh, Mr. Carter. Of course, come in. Have a seat. Just give me a few seconds to finish this. *(DANIEL sits. LOAN OFFICER taps keys on computer, then looks at DANIEL)* How have you been?

DANIEL

Pretty good. Well, truthfully, I've had a few bumps in the road. My wife – you met her when we took out the loan on our condo – found out she has cancer.

LOAN OFFICER

I'm so sorry to hear that. How's she doing?

DANIEL

She's fighting it.

LOAN OFFICER

Please extend my best wishes.

94

BROKEN SPIRIT

DANIEL

Thanks.

LOAN OFFICER

(Pause) We should take a look at your loan application. *(Pause)* Let's start with the basics. You and your wife, Jessica, own your house. It's appraised at $350,000. You have an annuity of $100,000. You purchased a waterfront condo two years ago for $250,000. You now owe $175,000. You have an outstanding balance in your three credit cards of about $45,000. Is that right?

DANIEL

Just one change. Since I completed the application, I added about $5,000 in credit card debt.

LOAN OFFICER

In one month?

DANIEL

That's for prescription drugs for my wife. We have to pay when we exceed the limit on my insurance.

LOAN OFFICER

Will that be every month going forward?

DANIEL

It'll be up to the doctor.

LOAN OFFICER

(Pause) What else is different?

DANIEL

Nothing major.

BROKEN SPIRIT

LOAN OFFICER
(Pause) I'd like to talk about what you've put down for the size of your loan request and how you plan to use it.

DANIEL
Jess needs a more aggressive treatment to beat it.

LOAN OFFICER
Doesn't your medical insurance cover it?

DANIEL
I'm afraid not. It's – um – experimental.

LOAN OFFICER
Did your doctor recommend this?

DANIEL
(Pause) The oncologist wants Jess to get better.

LOAN OFFICER
We normally wouldn't loan money to pay for medical treatment.

DANIEL
But I have a fully paid house worth $350,000.

LOAN OFFICER
You used your house as collateral to purchase your condo. Your wife is no longer earning a pay check – at least until she returns to work – and your credit card debts and remaining loan payments don't give you much 'wiggle room'. I'm sorry to give you this bad news, Mr. Carter. You've been a solid customer at our bank, and we like doing business with you. But on this particular request, I'm afraid we can't help you.

DANIEL
I can't let my wife --- Are you sure? The money will be used for a good purpose.

BROKEN SPIRIT

LOAN OFFICER

I wish we could help.

DANIEL

How about I tell you the money is going to be used --- to buy a boat --- or we're going to do some things to fix up our house?

LOAN OFFICER

You don't really plan to do that, right?

DANIEL

But say I did – you know, put that down on the application – wouldn't I then have a chance to get the money?

LOAN OFFICER

You don't have enough equity. *(Pause)* I'm not your financial advisor, but perhaps you might want to cash in your annuity.

DANIEL

I already thought of that. I can't without incurring a substantial penalty. I'd be throwing away money when I can least afford to do so.

LOAN OFFICER

You still have $50,000 available in your Equity Credit Line. As you know, this can be used for any purpose.

DANIEL

I'm going to need that money to pay for the prescription drugs.

LOAN OFFICER

When your wife returns to work, I can take another look at what I might be able to do, loan-wise.

DANIEL

When my wife and I were both working and our credit cards had almost no outstanding balances, you couldn't loan me enough. Don't you remember? I actually turned down taking out a larger loan. You bankers are all the same. When you need us, you climb mountains to hand out money. When the tables turn, it's "oh, no, Mr. Carter, come back when you don't really need the money, and we'll give you a garbage bag with loads of cash".

LOAN OFFICER

You know that's not true, Mr. Carter. We want to make loans, but there has to be enough equity.

DANIEL

What about loyalty to a longtime customer? What about your bank president asking me to serve on the Board of Directors? You know, I bet if I called him /

LOAN OFFICER

/ I spoke to him already.

DANIEL

When?

LOAN OFFICER

Yesterday. I showed him your loan application. I wanted to be sure he fully agreed with me in all respects.

DANIEL

We've played golf together a few times. He's met Jess. I can't believe he would say "no" to me.

LOAN OFFICER

Would you like to speak directly to him now?

BROKEN SPIRIT

DANIEL

Yes, I would. I can get this all straightened out and get the money my wife needs. He's on the fourth floor, right?

LOAN OFFICER

I was in his office less than an hour ago. He has a luncheon meeting across town. I assume he's in his car now. I could call his cellphone if you'd like.

DANIEL

That would be great. *(LOAN OFFICER dials number and hands cellphone to DANIEL)* Hello. This is Daniel Carter. I'm sorry to bother you. *(Pause)* But we should meet so I can fill you in on some details that aren't on the loan application. *(Pause)* It's critical. I mean it's really critical. *(Pause)* Can't you make an exception? We're friends; I've been a loyal customer of your bank for years; my wife's life depends on getting this. *(Long pause)* So, you're saying, "we're friends" and "my bank is always there for you" was just a lot of malarky? *(Pause)* I am calm! Why wouldn't I be? I not only don't get the money I need, but I also get told my friendship and loyalty are now passe. *(Pause)* Oh sure, I'll tell Jess that you said, "hi". When she asks if I got the money, I'll tell her that you think we don't need it – or what I should say – we don't have enough equity so you'd better get on with it – and die if you must. *(Ends phone call)* You're right. He agrees with you.

(BLACK OUT)

(END OF SCENE)

BROKEN SPIRIT

Scene 10

SETTING: ***Office of the Superintendent of Schools.***

AT RISE: ***NICOLE is sitting at her desk, and DANIEL is seated by her desk.***

DANIEL

That was the first time I saw the Mayor speak out so strongly against your budget.

NICOLE

He never has. As much as I pride myself on communicating well and understanding people's motives, I sometimes get ambushed.

DANIEL

We only got a 1.99 percent increase last year. He must realize that you'd have to make major cuts in staffing.

NICOLE

We have our marching orders.

DANIEL

ONE PERCENT!!! Insurance is higher; special education is higher; he knows about the contracted settlements. IT'S RIDICULOUS!!!

NICOLE

I know you're under a lot of pressure.

DANIEL

You know if I won the lottery /

BROKEN SPIRIT

NICOLE

/ We don't have the luxury of venting. We've got to put together a budget that the Mayor and Board of Education will support.

DANIEL

I apologize.

NICOLE

When the budget is put to bed, I insist you take some vacation time.

DANIEL

I know I've been --- I won't let you down.

NICOLE

Close the door, please. *(DANIEL closes the door)* I need to talk to you. I've been reluctant to do it before we finish with our budget. But things are getting a little out of hand.

DANIEL

I'm sorry I snapped at you just now.

NICOLE

If that's all there was, we wouldn't be having this conversation. When you took the day off last week, your staff asked to speak to me.

DANIEL

I know I've been a little short, sometimes. But there's a lot to do.

NICOLE

We've worked together for about three years. You've had enormous pressure to accomplish so much. Yet, the staff always raved about how wonderful it was to work for you. Now it's different.

DANIEL

I've had a few down-moments.

NICOLE

You need to function like you've always done. I'm truly sorry about Jessica, and whatever else has fallen in your lap. But I've got to make sure all of my staff – especially my top administrator – is performing at their best.

DANIEL

I understand.

NICOLE

(Long pause) You let me share with you some private frustrations with my divorce. If you feel the need /

DANIEL

/ It's a struggle. *(Pause)* We talked about selling our condo.

NICOLE

You should probably get a good price for it.

DANIEL

It's too late.

NICOLE

Why?

DANIEL

There was a fire caused by a faulty electrical panel.

NICOLE

In your condo?

DANIEL

No. I replaced mine, right after it was inspected. But nobody else wanted to spend the money. All the units have the same 1980's electrical panel. *(Continued)*

DANIEL (Continued)

With the ocean nearby, there's always going to be a lot of corrosion. A fire started in another apartment in the building. We have to pay a special assessment for the damage to the 'common areas'.

NICOLE

Do you know how much?

DANIEL

Not yet, but that's not the half of it. The Homeowners Association's Board of Directors put off repairing the pilings under the building. A structural engineer said we should replace the rotten ones within a year. That was almost a year and a half ago.

NICOLE

I'm afraid to ask what happened?

DANIEL

Purchasing the condo was a big mistake.

NICOLE

Don't be so hard on yourself.

DANIEL

The building shifted just a little. Again, nothing was done. "Hold off on spending any money", that's their go-to position.

NICOLE

You're talking about the Board of Directors, right?

DANIEL

Yeah. *(Pause)* Dues haven't been raised in five years!!! The Reserve Account is depleted.

BROKEN SPIRIT

NICOLE

You worked part of your career in banking. I'm sure you thought of borrowing the money.

DANIEL

We haven't done any independent financial audits for years. You need at least the last three years of audits to borrow.

NICOLE

What about insurance? Your Board must have purchased it.

DANIEL

The insurance policy doesn't cover items that are due to poor maintenance. In fact, all liability related to the pilings is not covered.

NICOLE

Let's hope you don't have a major collapse of your condo building.

DANIEL

Luckily, I set up an LLC. Thank goodness I did. At least I would only lose my investment in the condo if worse came to worse.

NICOLE

I wish I could offer you some constructive suggestions. But you're the financial expert. *(Pause)* You need to take heed of what I said earlier. I need you to control your emotions.

DANIEL

I'll try to do better.

NICOLE

Do more than just try.

(BLACK OUT)

BROKEN SPIRIT

BROKEN SPIRIT

Scene 11

SETTING: ***The Bar.***

AT RISE: ***DANIEL on bar stool***
looking at the audience.

DANIEL

The next month --- well, nothing seemed to go right. *(Lights out on bar and lights up on the Carter's living room. One month earlier)*

DANIEL

(JESSICA is lying on the sofa. DANIEL enters the scene. He has a glass of whiskey in his hand. A half-filled bottle of whiskey sits on the nearby end table. JESSICA is watching DANIEL)

JESSICA

You hardly ever drank until I got sick.

DANIEL

There's nothing to worry about. It helps me relax. *(Long pause)* I was thinking about the day I asked you to marry me. I was so nervous. I had practiced my little speech in front of the mirror. I had written it out and memorized it. When the big moment came, I got down on my knee, took out the engagement ring, and started to talk. An airplane happened to go over head and the noise was too loud to continue. So I paused to wait until it got quiet again.

JESSICA

I liked it much better when you said those things extemporaneously. Your sense of humor kicked in. I loved your entreaty, "please don't serve me beets". Like I would ever do that. I know what you like and don't like.

BROKEN SPIRIT

DANIEL

We didn't have much money then. You made your own clothes. You spent money wisely. Nobody can shop better than you.

JESSICA

And you always have hated shopping.

DANIEL

There's been a lot of good times.

JESSICA

Yes, there has.

DANIEL

I'm not going to give up trying.

JESSICA

What can I do to help you?

DANIEL

Get better. Make all of this go away.

JESSICA

Some things can't be controlled. But our love and respect for one another will always be there. We're partners for life.

DANIEL

I feel the same about you.

JESSICA

I know my time is running out. I'm afraid of what's going to happen to you.

DANIEL

I'm supposed to worry about you.

BROKEN SPIRIT

JESSICA

Everything possible has been done.

DANIEL

There is the experimental therapy.

JESSICA

You heard what Dr. Holt said, "there's no indication it works". We'd be wasting money for something that hasn't proved its worth.

DANIEL

But we don't know that for sure. If I had secured the finances, like I'm supposed to do, we could have TRIED it. You never know about these things.

JESSICA

You've always felt confident in your decision-making. Now you're doubting yourself.

DANIEL

How are you feeling?

JESSICA

I won't lie. I don't feel well. It's getting worse. We both know where things are headed.

DANIEL

I'm not going to give up trying.

JESSICA

Would you make me a promise?

DANIEL

Sure. Anything.

BROKEN SPIRIT

JESSICA

Please stop the drinking.

DANIEL

I will. I promise you. But you've got to understand, it helps me relax, to sleep better, to function better. I'm not drinking much. And I can stop, anytime I want. You only see me at times like this when I'm feeling a little down. But our talk has really given me the inspiration I need. You always make me feel better.

JESSICA

I need to rest. You can go ahead and microwave the leftovers from yesterday whenever you want to eat supper. Can you do that?

DANIEL

Sure, go ahead and rest. *(JESSICA lays her head on the pillow; DANIEL covers her with a blanket; JESSICA falls asleep quickly. DANIEL fills his glass again with liquor, goes to drink it, hesitates, then drinks it)*

(BLACK OUT)

(END OF SCENE)

BROKEN SPIRIT

Scene 12

SETTING: *Office of the Superintendent of Schools.*

AT RISE: *NICOLE is sitting at her desk, and DANIEL is seated by her desk. The office door is closed.*

DANIEL

I know why you want to see me. It's about what happened at the Board of Education meeting yesterday. I shouldn't have been so curt to the Board Chair. He just was getting on my nerves. But then, I know, I should've kept my cool. Of course, he got angry and said things that embarrassed me. So, what could I do? I had to respond. Didn't I? If I stayed silent, he would have had the upper hand.

NICOLE

Your numbers didn't add up. I've never seen so many mistakes. Didn't you check it?

DANIEL

It's my staff. They're all incompetent.

NICOLE

Even if they're as bad as you say, you're still responsible.

DANIEL

I do the work of ten people! You've always said I'm your best hire. Of course, there's been some stress. I've always handled it. You've seen me do it time and time again, right?

NICOLE

I smell liquor. Have you been drinking?

DANIEL
Yeah, last night at home. Is that against the rules?

NICOLE
Why has it all gone so wrong with you? I know Jessica has been very ill. That would be hard for anybody to take. I understand that has to be very difficult.

DANIEL
Jess has been my rock.

NICOLE
Talking in an unprofessional manner to your staff, other administrators and teachers, the public, let alone Board Members, is just not acceptable. But drinking on the job, well, you know as well I do, that's an offense we can't tolerate in a school district.

DANIEL
You encouraged me to take some vacation time. So I'll take it now. One week of rest and relaxation and then I'll come back all refreshed.

NICOLE
I've given you multiple warnings. You've received formal reprimands. You're good for a day or two, but then you go off the rails. Your drinking is noticeable. In the past week alone, over a dozen people have complained to me about your behavior.

DANIEL
I don't know who called or stopped by. But I'm sure they had an axe to grind against me. I probably didn't approve a purchase order; or maybe it was a parent who wanted their child's bus stop changed and I refused; or who knows? Some people complain about everything. You know the type. Why blame me for their insecurities? I'm the best hire you've made. How many times have you told me?

NICOLE

(NICOLE picks up a folder and takes out a letter) I'm going to give you the professional courtesy of having a choice. I have here a letter – which has been written by the Board Attorney and authorized by the Board of Education at its executive session last night – you can resign immediately. You will be paid for all of your unused vacation days – there are twenty-three – and half of your unused sick leave – sixty-one days. Also, the Board has agreed to provide one year of medical, dental, and prescription drug coverage for you and your wife at no cost.

DANIEL

What's the alternative?

NICOLE

I fire you, effective today. You will receive your unused vacation pay. Nothing more. No payment for half your unused sick leave; no insurance, except for what you pay for on your own.

DANIEL

How can you do this to me? I've been the most loyal and trustworthy administrator you have. Doesn't that count for anything?

NICOLE

It's been your good work before things changed, that the Board of Education took into consideration. That's why they made this generous offer. So, here's the letter for you to read. Before you leave my office, you'll need to decide. You can sign the letter and get the severance package. Or you can walk out of here without it. I encourage you to sign. It's your best option.

DANIEL

(DANIEL doesn't read the letter but signs it) Here, you've got your blood! May I say "goodbye" to my staff?

NICOLE

I don't think that would be a good idea. They're rightfully upset, and you'll only make matters worse. I've alerted the Security Guard. He should be waiting outside my door. He'll escort you to your car in the parking lot. You should leave your keys and security card with me.

DANIEL

(DANIEL fumbles for his keys and security card and gives them to NICOLE) What about my personal things in my office?

NICOLE

The Head Custodian was also alerted. All of your personal things have been boxed up. All the boxes will be brought out to your car. If you find something missing, just call me and I will make sure it is delivered to your home. Do you have any other questions?

DANIEL

I made a few errors. I got a few people upset. I drink, a little. Nobody's perfect.

NICOLE

I wish you well.

DANIEL

If that was true, you wouldn't be doing this to me.

NICOLE

I'm truly sorry for all you have endured. I hope – I really hope – things turn around for you. *(Pause)* You'll have all of your health insurance coverage for a year. There are therapy sessions for mental health, and you'll find options for getting help with your drinking problem.

DANIEL

(Long pause) I never thought this would happen. *(Pause)* My computer password is 97AR45. I appreciate all you've done for me. *(DANIEL rises from seat, looks at NICOLE as if to say something else, then exits)*

(BLACK OUT)

(END OF SCENE)

BROKEN SPIRIT

Scene 13

SETTING: *Carter's backyard.*
Door to kitchen. One
week earlier.

AT RISE: *DANIEL is cooking at*
the grill. JESSICA is in
a wheelchair. JASON is
setting up the picnic
table for the barbeque.

DANIEL

Finally, we have a chance to take a break. No job. No work. No responsibilities. *(DANIEL takes a drink of whiskey)* And you, my dear, can sit and relax. No need to get anything. Jason and I have things under control.

JASON

Where's the mustard? I didn't see any in the refrigerator.

JESSICA

Look in the pantry. Second shelf. Probably on the left side, maybe behind something. *(JASON goes to kitchen)*

DANIEL

You need to take it easy. Jason and I are perfectly capable of doing this.

JASON

(JASON enters with a jar of mustard and a jar of pickles) I found the mustard, and I also found pickles. Do we have chips?

JESSICA

They're in the cabinet, to the left of the stove.

JASON

I'll get them. *(JASON exits again)*

DANIEL

(To JESSICA) Are you sure you don't want to eat something? There has to be something you'd like.

JESSICA

(To DANIEL) I'm not hungry. *(Pause)* I'm feeling chilly. Could you get me a blanket?

DANIEL

Would you like for us to eat indoors? *(DANIEL drinks more whiskey)*

JESSICA

No, just need a blanket to keep warm.

DANIEL

(JASON enters with chips) I'm getting Jess a blanket. Could you watch the grill? *(DANIEL exits)*

JASON

(To JESSICA) You don't have to be cold. We can go inside.

JESSICA

Daniel already offered. I'm fine here. Just a little chill. That's all. I'm sure it'll pass.

JASON

I'm worried, Jess. Are you sure you're okay?

JESSICA

It's just ---

<h1 style="text-align:center">BROKEN SPIRIT</h1>

DANIEL
(DANIEL enters with two blankets and puts the blankets gently on JESSICA) Here, sweetheart. Are you sure you don't want to go inside?

JESSICA
Thanks. *(DANIEL gets on his knee and holds JESSICA's hand)* Are you going to propose?

DANIEL
You look so --- fragile. Are you sure /

JESSICA
Now stop worrying.

DANIEL
You're right. *(DANIEL adjusts the blanket on JESSICA, and she falls asleep)*

JASON
(Pause) Did you finally get the insurance check for the car accident?

DANIEL
Yeah.

JASON
So, all your worrying about getting the money wasn't necessary.

DANIEL
They paid half.

JASON
Of the total loss?

DANIEL
Yeah.

BROKEN SPIRIT

JASON

You've been through so much.

DANIEL

You can say that again.

JASON

(Pause) Do you want to borrow some money?

DANIEL

Are you the new local bank?

JASON

I'm just trying to help my best friend.

DANIEL

(Long pause) I tried.

JASON

What're you talking about?

DANIEL

I went to the bank – the same guy who told me only a couple of years ago I could borrow all I needed to purchase the condo – now my credit's no good.

JASON

I'm sorry I brought it up.

DANIEL

(Pause) Sometimes I just feel like there's a black cloud hanging over me. I just get so upset – well, take for instance our paperboy. I like to get up, dress, and eat breakfast while I'm reading the newspaper. *(Continued)*

DANIEL (Continued)
I'm probably one of only a hundred people in the universe that actually buys a paper instead of using an app. Anyway, for three days in a row last week, the paper came after I had my breakfast. Is that just a coincidence, bad luck, or what?

JASON
That's just over the top. If it's going to bother you so much, buy the app. You can read it whenever.

DANIEL
That's not my point. Things seem to get in my way. I was headed to work. I usually go down Pine Road, but just for a change of pace, I went down Hubble Court. I was curious to see this new house they're building. Anyway, I got stuck behind a school bus. You won't believe this, but it tied up traffic for almost ten minutes.

JASON
Why?

DANIEL
The bus driver stopped to pick up this boy. He got on the bus then ran off the bus and went into his house. His mother came out and talked with the bus driver. A few minutes later the boy came out again. I was so annoyed I called the school as soon as I got to work. Do you know what they told me? This kid had to vomit. And the mother asked the bus driver to wait for him. Why hold up the bus? An even better question is: Why did the mother let her sick son go to school?

JASON
You're making mountains out of mole hills.

DANIEL
Jess wanted me to pick up milk /

BROKEN SPIRIT

JASON

/ Oh, for Heaven's sake, please stop. You're making yourself crazy. Calm down. *(DANIEL's cellphone rings; JESSICA stirs)* I think that's your phone.

DANIEL

(DANIEL puts his cellphone to his ear) Hello. *(Pause)* I'm having a barbeque with my wife and friend. Is it important? *(To JESSICA)* It's our condo president. *(To caller)* I'm listening. *(Long pause)*

JESSICA

Is everything alright? *(DANIEL continues listening to caller, very intensely)* What's wrong?

DANIEL

That's all on you and your Board of Directors! *(Pause)* No. No. No. You all knew about it for months. *(Pause)* Of course, I'm upset. And I'm not going to "tone it down". You and your cheapskate bunch of morons let this happen!!! *(Pause)* No, you shut up. I warned all of you – over and over, again and again – "what was it going to take", I asked, and you know what I heard? *(Pause)* You've got to be kidding. I said, "get it done before we have a catastrophe". *(DANIEL rubs his left arm)* Stop making stuff up --- *(DANIEL is short of breath)* Get real. That's been the problem --- Oh *(DANIEL drops the cellphone)* I can't breath --- help me --- *(DANIEL collapses)*

JESSICA

Oh my God!

JASON

(JASON dials 911 on cell phone) We need an ambulance right away.

(BLACK OUT)

(END OF SCENE)

BROKEN SPIRIT

<u>Scene 14</u>

SETTING: *Hospital Room.*

AT RISE: *DANIEL is in the bed.*
                                                 JASON is sitting.

DANIEL

Is Jess coming?

JASON

She wanted to, but the doctor advised against it.

DANIEL

They're making me stay a couple more days. Like that's going to make
any difference.

JASON

Your drinking needs to stop.

DANIEL

Quit talking about that. I've heard you. Enough already.

JASON

What did the doctor say?

DANIEL

My blood pressure is too high.

JASON

And?

DANIEL

Let's change the subject, or I'll have another heart attack.

JASON

(Pause) When you're up to it, I'll set up a foursome.

DANIEL

You think you'll have an advantage. I don't plan to hit as many balls into that pond on the course. By the way, how many golf balls do they usually find in the water, each month?

JASON

I have no idea.

DANIEL

Guess.

JASON

Don't tell me you know the answer.

DANIEL

Of course, I do.

JASON

No way.

DANIEL

145.

JASON

Are you making the number up?

DANIEL

I spoke to the Groundskeeper. He showed me the buckets of balls. You can buy them at a discount. I asked him if I could count the balls marked with a "D" – my personal identification mark. Guess how many?

JASON

145.

DANIEL

No. 35. It was a record of some kind, I'm sure.

JASON

I remember the first time you played golf. It was raining at the start.
You were wearing glasses at the time. You complained your glasses
were fogged up and that's why the ball was going in all directions but
the right one. You even hit one ball from the tee on the fifteen hole
right onto the green for the sixteenth hole. And what was your score
for eighteen holes?

DANIEL

169.

JASON

You actually got a plaque for that.

DANIEL

"WORST GOLFER". I had it hanging on my office wall – it's at home
now – alongside my "CONNECTICUT SCHOOL BUSINESS
OFFICIAL OF THE YEAR" plaque.

JASON

(NICOLE enters) Hey, Nicole. I didn't know you were coming.

NICOLE

Jessica called me. *(To DANIEL)* I hope you don't mind me being
here.

DANIEL

I honestly appreciate it.

BROKEN SPIRIT

NICOLE

How are you feeling?

DANIEL

I hope to get released in a couple of days. Jess is home, as you probably know. I'm anxious to see her.

NICOLE

I have a card here. It's signed by the district office staff. They all hope you recover quickly.

DANIEL

Tell them I really appreciate their kindness.

JASON

(To NICOLE) I was telling Daniel we were going to play golf when he's up to it. Would you like to join us?

NICOLE

I'll take a pass. I'm terrible at golf.

DANIEL

Not as bad as I am.

NICOLE

My game is bowling.

JASON

Oh my, I forgot how bad Daniel is at that game, too. He might hold the record for the most gutter balls in a single season. *(To DANIEL)* Do you?

DANIEL

I haven't yet been given that honor, but there's always the possibility I will achieve that goal.

BROKEN SPIRIT

NICOLE
I'm so glad to see you with your sense of humor.

DANIEL
Tranquilizers. They work wonders.

NICOLE
I'm going to your house after I leave here. Is there anything you want me to say to Jessica?

DANIEL
(Long pause) Forgive me.

NICOLE
I'll tell her that you love her and miss her.

DANIEL
Of course.

NICOLE
I wanted to stop by to give you that card and see how you're doing.

DANIEL
I really appreciate it.

JASON
(NICOLE exits) I'll be right back. *(Jason exits. NURSE enters)*

NURSE
How are you doing today, Mr. Carter?

DANIEL
I wish you'd call me Daniel.

NURSE
No problem, Daniel. I've brought your pills.

124

BROKEN SPIRIT

DANIEL

Did the doctor change what I can eat?

NURSE

There's nothing changed on your chart.

DANIEL

I've heard it said that the hospital food is what gets the patients to want to leave as quickly as possible.

NURSE

It could also be the cost.

DANIEL

(Long pause) Yeah. You're probably right. *(JASON enters)* This is my best friend – Jason Lewis. He's single. Plays a great game of golf. And he thinks I'm too weak to beat him when we play again.

NURSE

(To JASON) It's nice to meet you. *(To DANIEL)* You can use your call button if you need any assistance. *(NURSE exits)*

DANIEL

Cute, huh? What do you think?

JASON

Stop. *(Pause)* You've got to be getting better. You're back to trying to fix me up, like Jessica.

DANIEL

(Long pause) I'm worried.

JASON

I know you are.

125

DANIEL

I don't know what I'm going to do.

JASON

You're going to try to relax. Get yourself back to where you can go home. Then you'll do what is necessary. You've always done that.

DANIEL

This time it's different.

(BLACK OUT)

(END OF SCENE)

BROKEN SPIRIT

Scene 15

SETTING: ***Bar room with two
stools. Present.***

AT RISE: ***DANIEL and JASON
are sitting. CHRIS is
standing.***

CHRIS

(To JASON) What can I get you?

JASON

A glass of seltzer. No ice.

DANIEL

If you came to give me a lecture, I'm not in the mood.

JASON

I've already tried that.

DANIEL

Why did you come here?

JASON

I have something for you. *(JASON takes an envelope from his pocket
and puts it on the bar counter in front of DANIEL)*

DANIEL

What's in that? An eviction notice from the bar?

JASON

It's a note from Jessica.

DANIEL

(Long pause) She wrote it /

127

BROKEN SPIRIT

JASON

/ While you were being taken to the hospital.

DANIEL

(Long pause) I'm glad you were with her.

JASON

(Nods) -

DANIEL

Do you know what she wrote?

JASON

No.

DANIEL

I'm sure I know. "Daniel, don't drink anymore. Daniel, get back to living. Daniel, be strong, like you've always been."

JASON

What would be wrong with saying those things?

DANIEL

I failed to get her the treatment she needed. I'm fifty years old. I'm unemployed. Do you think that note is going to make it all go away?

JASON

You know I drank a lot. But I'm a recovering alcoholic. One day at a time.

DANIEL

Ah, I see where you're going with this. You want to carpool with me. We can go together to those AA meetings.

JASON

(Long pause) Do you remember Mary Graves?

DANIEL

Um, not really – wait! Yes, I do. She was the lead in the school play.
Wasn't she in one of your classes?

JASON

Yeah. Introduction to Acting. She wanted to become a professional
actress. I took the class because I thought it would be easy.

DANIEL

Why do you mention her?

JASON

I ran into her. She mentioned that she was starring in a play at the
Randle Theater. She had only kind words about you.

DANIEL

That's nice to hear. I had a minor role in a play we were in. I helped
her learn her lines.

JASON

She also told me something else.

DANIEL

What?

JASON

Mary told me that she felt totally abandoned when her boyfriend - who
she thought would become her husband – said he found another girl. It
really threw her for a loop. But you were the one who gave her sound
advice. Mary trusted you.

DANIEL

I guess I did help her.

BROKEN SPIRIT

JASON

Mary told me that she is happily married. She had a lot of insecurities,
but you were her rock when she needed a friend to talk to.

DANIEL

Why do you bring that up?

JASON

Mary talked about your strength of character. It's the same way Jessica
felt about you. The drinking serves no purpose. It just brings you down
more.

DANIEL

I think Jess was disappointed in me.

JASON

You're wrong.

DANIEL

I've become a drunk without a job.

JASON

You used to take things in stride.

DANIEL

Losing Jess – was just too much.

JASON

We all face obstacles every day. Some are small, and some are huge.
I'm not saying it's easy. Look at me. I totally fell apart when Molly
left me. I drank a lot and took drugs. I'm no role model for how to
handle a tough situation.

DANIEL

But you managed.

BROKEN SPIRIT

JASON

I got a kick in the pants from Nicole. She told me that I had to get help before I could go on teaching.

DANIEL

And you're saying /

JASON

/ Nicole did you a favor, in a way, by giving you a 'wakeup call'. You screwed up and made things impossible. But you have the insurance to get the help you need.

DANIEL

So what am I supposed to do? Go to rehab. Go back to Nicole and beg for my job.

JASON

You should go to rehab. But it's not likely you can get back the CFO job at the school.

DANIEL

So, why try?

JASON

Your life is not over. There are other things you can do. You haven't been convicted of a crime. You're a certified public accountant. Nicole told me that she's willing to write a job recommendation for you.

DANIEL

She really said that?

JASON

Read the note.

131

BROKEN SPIRIT

DANIEL

(DANIEL picks up the envelope, hesitates, then crumples it and throws it back on the bar counter) What's there to say? I'm not going to be anything more than what I am now. I've lost my way. The one person who could've help me isn't here. *(CHRIS moves back into the shadows and is replaced by JESSICA, looking as young, healthy, and beautiful as the day DANIEL first met her)*

JESSICA

You told me yourself, "love is an unbroken bond". I'm always going to be in your heart and mind. Do you remember the music box you gave me for our first anniversary? The one that I accidently broke. You held my hand and told me that the tune would be in my mind whenever I wanted to hear it. And it was. Maybe you remember the bouquet of roses you bought for me on our tenth anniversary. One of the roses didn't open. And I wondered if this was some sort of bad omen. You said, "watch a little longer", and the next day that rose opened wide. When my mother died, you brought me out into our backyard, and we sat there looking up at the stars. Then we saw a shooting star. You asked if that could possibly be my mom. You never insisted it was, but your calm, soothing voice reassured me that there will be a reunion of souls in the afterlife. *(JESSICA looks at the envelope)* There's always truth to be found in the words of a loved one. *(DANIEL picks up the envelope, takes out the note and reads it, as JESSICA moves back into the shadows, replaced by CHRIS. DANIEL begins to speak before he looks up)*

DANIEL

Jess, I ---

CHRIS

Did you say something?

DANIEL

No, I guess not. *(Pause) (To JASON)* Let's go.

CHRIS

Wait a second! *(CHRIS hands DANIEL his wristwatch)* This is yours. The drinks were a loan. Pay me back when you can.

DANIEL

Thanks. This watch means a lot to me.

JASON

(DANIEL and JASON stand) Are you going to tell me what Jessica wrote?

DANIEL

(DANIEL puts his arm on JASON's shoulder as they leave the bar) Jess wrote the greatest words a man can hear from his wife.

JASON

"I love you"?

DANIEL

Better. "I believe in you".

(DANIEL and JASON exit into the shadows. CHRIS wipes down the bar as the light slowly fades to black)

(BLACK OUT)

(END OF PLAY)